Don't be Afraid, Just Be

Copyright© Vanessa Ingrid Health & Wellness Coaching, LLC.
All rights reserved. No parts of this publication may be reproduced without written permission

Vanessa Ingrid Health & Wellness Coaching, LLC.
PO Box 3275
Frederiksted, St. Croix
United States Virgin Islands (USVI)
00841-3275
www.vihealthcoaching.com

Scripture marked KJV are from the Holy Bible, King James Version. All rights reserved.

Scriptures marked NIV are taken from the NEW INTERNATIONAL VERSION®, NIV® Copyright © 1973, 1978, 1984, 2011 by Biblica, Inc.® Used by permission. All rights reserved worldwide.

ISBN Hardcover: 978-1-7350704-4-5

Don't be Afraid Just Believe

As a woman, there is much on your shoulders to bear
But the Lord is faithful to handle every care
Whether duties at home or in the workplace
Sufficient is God's strength, and perfect is His grace

You're ability to conquer the hardships of life
Is dependent on your leaning into the strength of Christ
God's provision is abundant so **don't be afraid**
He is faithful to answer every prayer you've prayed

You don't need to have everything figured out
And may experience occasional feelings of doubt
Never forget how awesome you are
You are one of a kind and you set your own bar

Take time for yourself every now and then
For as sure as Jesus is Lord, the sun will shine again
Ask for strength and **just believe** He will carry you through
May God bless the fruits of your labor and everything you do

This Prayer Journal Belongs to:

TODAY'S DATE: /   /

"Don't be afraid; just believe."
Mark 5:36 NIV

_____
_____
_____
_____
_____
_____
_____
_____
_____
_____
_____
_____
_____
_____
_____
_____
_____
_____
_____
_____
_____
_____
_____
_____
_____

TODAY'S DATE: /   /

TODAY'S DATE: / /

*"On days of weeping,
may worship and praise be your weapon."*

TODAY'S DATE: / /

TODAY'S DATE: /   /

"Do not be anxious about anything, but in every situation, by prayer and petition, with thanksgiving, present your requests to God." **Philippians 4:6 NIV**

TODAY'S DATE: /   /

TODAY'S DATE: / /

"Our weakness is an opportunity for the perfection of God's strength within us to shine."

TODAY'S DATE: /   /

TODAY'S DATE: /   /

"'If you can'?" said Jesus.
"Everything is possible for one who believes."
Mark 9:23 NIV

TODAY'S DATE: /   /

TODAY'S DATE: /   /

*"God will hold you together even
when you feel like you are falling apart."*

TODAY'S DATE: /   /

TODAY'S DATE: / /

"If you believe, you will receive whatever you ask for in prayer." **Matthew 21:22 NIV**

_____
_____
_____
_____
_____
_____
_____
_____
_____
_____
_____
_____
_____
_____
_____
_____
_____
_____
_____
_____
_____
_____
_____

TODAY'S DATE: /   /

TODAY'S DATE: /   /

"Your cry for help is God's cue for consolation."

TODAY'S DATE: /   /

TODAY'S DATE: / /

"Now therefore fear ye not; I will nourish you and your little ones." And he comforted them, and spoke kindly unto them." **Genesis 50:21 KJV**

TODAY'S DATE: / /

TODAY'S DATE: / /

*"Fear is just a feeling.
Feelings are gauges, not guides - so, trust God and chill."*

TODAY'S DATE: / /

TODAY'S DATE: /   /

"And my God will supply every need of yours according to his riches in glory in Christ Jesus."
Philippians 4:19 KJV

TODAY'S DATE: /   /

TODAY'S DATE: /   /

"Stop "hanging in" and start "holding on" to God. He can be trusted on your darkest day."

TODAY'S DATE: /   /

TODAY'S DATE: / /

"For His anger endureth but a moment, and in His favor is life; weeping may endure for a night, but joy cometh in the morning." **Psalm 30:5 KJV**

___
___
___
___
___
___
___
___
___
___
___
___
___
___
___
___
___
___
___
___
___
___
___
___

TODAY'S DATE: /   /

TODAY'S DATE: /   /

"Let the nervousness in your gut be the humble reminder of your deep need for God."

TODAY'S DATE: /   /

TODAY'S DATE: / /

"In God I will praise his word, in God I have put my trust; I will not fear what flesh can do unto me."
Psalm 56:4 KJV

TODAY'S DATE: / /

TODAY'S DATE: /   /

"To lead, you must first be aware of your own need—for fun, family, and fellowship."

TODAY'S DATE: / /

TODAY'S DATE: / /

"Neither height nor depth, nor anything else in all creation, will be able to separate us from the love of God that is in Christ Jesus our Lord."
Romans 8:39 NIV

TODAY'S DATE: / /

TODAY'S DATE: / /

"At the end of every day, unplug from stress, plug in to rest, and repeat."

TODAY'S DATE: / /

TODAY'S DATE: /   /

*"So we fix our eyes not on what is seen,
but on what is unseen, since what is seen is temporary,
but what is unseen is eternal."* **2 Corinthians 4:18 NIV**

_____
_____
_____
_____
_____
_____
_____
_____
_____
_____
_____
_____
_____
_____
_____
_____
_____
_____
_____
_____
_____
_____
_____
_____
_____

TODAY'S DATE: / /

TODAY'S DATE: /   /

*"Playing small doesn't make you humble.
False humility is still disobedience to God."*

TODAY'S DATE: /   /

TODAY'S DATE: / /

"Now faith is confidence in what we hope for and assurance about what we do not see."
Hebrews 11:1 NIV

TODAY'S DATE: / /

TODAY'S DATE: / /

*"No one can benefit from your untapped potential.
Live to die empty."*

TODAY'S DATE: /   /

TODAY'S DATE: /   /

"He that dwelleth in the secret place of the most High shall abide under the shadow of the Almighty."
Psalm 91:1 KJV

TODAY'S DATE: /   /

TODAY'S DATE: /   /

"The breath in your lungs is God's investment in you to achieve His purpose. Do what he called you to do."

TODAY'S DATE: /   /

TODAY'S DATE: / /

*"A thousand shall fall at thy side,
and ten thousand at thy right hand;
but it shall not come nigh thee."* **Psalm 91:7 KJV**

TODAY'S DATE:　　/　　/

TODAY'S DATE: /   /

*"Don't perform to prove who you already are—
you are fearfully and wonderfully made."*

_____
_____
_____
_____
_____
_____
_____
_____
_____
_____
_____
_____
_____
_____
_____
_____
_____
_____
_____
_____
_____
_____
_____

TODAY'S DATE: / /

TODAY'S DATE: /   /

*He says, "Be still, and know that I am God;
I will be exalted among the nations,
I will be exalted in the earth."* **Psalm 46:10 NIV**

TODAY'S DATE:　　/　　/

TODAY'S DATE: / /

"Whether responsibilities at home or in the workplace, sufficient is God strength, and perfect is His grace."

_____
_____
_____
_____
_____
_____
_____
_____
_____
_____
_____
_____
_____
_____
_____
_____
_____
_____
_____
_____
_____
_____

TODAY'S DATE: /   /

TODAY'S DATE: / /

"Be joyful in hope, patient in affliction, faithful in prayer."
Romans 12:12 NIV

TODAY'S DATE: / /

TODAY'S DATE: / /

*"God's provision is abundant so no need to be afraid,
He is faithful to respond to every prayer you've prayed."*

TODAY'S DATE: /   /

TODAY'S DATE: /   /

"And we know that in all things God works for good of those who love him, who have been called according to his purpose." **Romans 8:28 NIV**

_____
_____
_____
_____
_____
_____
_____
_____
_____
_____
_____
_____
_____
_____
_____
_____
_____
_____
_____
_____
_____
_____
_____

TODAY'S DATE: / /

TODAY'S DATE: / /

*"Your ability to conquer the hardships of work and home life,
is dependent on your leaning into the strength of Christ."*

TODAY'S DATE: /   /

TODAY'S DATE: /   /

"I can do all this through him who gives me strength."
Philippians 4:13 NIV

TODAY'S DATE: / /

TODAY'S DATE: / /

"Busyness and burn out are not badges of honor in God's sight – it's ok to ask for help."

_____
_____
_____
_____
_____
_____
_____
_____
_____
_____
_____
_____
_____
_____
_____
_____
_____
_____
_____
_____
_____
_____
_____
_____

TODAY'S DATE: / /

TODAY'S DATE: / /

"And the peace of God, which transcends all understanding, will guard your hearts and your minds in Christ Jesus."
Philippians 4:7 NIV

TODAY'S DATE: / /

TODAY'S DATE: /   /

"Your service to others is only as good as your self-care."

TODAY'S DATE: /   /

TODAY'S DATE: / /

"I praise you because I am fearfully and wonderfully made; your works are wonderful, I know that full well."
Psalm 139:14 NIV

TODAY'S DATE: /   /

TODAY'S DATE: /   /

"Ask God for guidance to determine whether you are still running in the right lane or the right race."

TODAY'S DATE: /   /

TODAY'S DATE: / /

"Though an army besiege me, my heart will not fear; though war break out against me, even then I will be confident." **Psalm 27:3 NIV**

TODAY'S DATE: / /

TODAY'S DATE: /   /

*"If you are too tired, you can't think.
Sleep is plenty productive – even Jesus rested."*

TODAY'S DATE: /   /

TODAY'S DATE: /   /

*"I sought the Lord, and he answered me;
he delivered me from all my fears."* **Psalm 34:4 NIV**

TODAY'S DATE: / /

TODAY'S DATE: / /

*"There will always be something to do,
so you can't afford to become undone."*

TODAY'S DATE: / /

TODAY'S DATE: /   /

"There is no fear in love. But perfect love drives out fear, because fear has to do with punishment. The one who fears is not made perfect in love."
1 John 4:18 NIV

TODAY'S DATE: /   /

TODAY'S DATE: / /

*"Without health, you are no help,
so make taking care of your temple a priority."*

TODAY'S DATE: / /

TODAY'S DATE: /   /

"For God so loved the world that he gave his one and only Son, that whoever believes in him shall not perish but have eternal life" **John 3:16 NIV**

TODAY'S DATE: /   /

TODAY'S DATE: /   /

*"Jobs are negotiable, sanity is not.
Take care of your mental health
by renewing your mind and thinking."*

TODAY'S DATE: / /

TODAY'S DATE: /   /

"For we live by faith, not by sight."
2 Corinthians 5:7 NIV

TODAY'S DATE: /   /

TODAY'S DATE: /   /

*"Take time for yourself every now and then,
for as sure as Jesus is Lord, the sun will shine again."*

TODAY'S DATE: / /

TODAY'S DATE: /   /

"For the Spirit God gave us does not make us timid, but gives us power, love and self-discipline."
2 Timothy 1:7 NIV

TODAY'S DATE: / /

TODAY'S DATE: / /

"Boundaries are the trademark of a balanced woman, ask God to help you establish and maintain healthy boundaries."

TODAY'S DATE: / /

TODAY'S DATE: / /

"Be kind and compassionate to one another, forgiving each other, just as in Christ God forgave you."
Ephesians 4:32 NIV

TODAY'S DATE: /   /

TODAY'S DATE: / /

*"Your sister is not your enemy.
There is enough space at the table for you both to win."*

TODAY'S DATE: /   /

TODAY'S DATE: / /

"But when you ask, you must believe and not doubt, because the one who doubts is like a wave of the sea, blown and tossed by the wind."
James 1:6 NIV

TODAY'S DATE: / /

TODAY'S DATE: /   /

"Playing it safe doesn't make you secure – it keeps you stuck. Take the leap of faith – God's got you!"

TODAY'S DATE: /   /

TODAY'S DATE: / /

"For I know the plans I have for you," declares the Lord, "plans to prosper you and not to harm you, plans to give you hope and a future."
Jerimiah 29:11 NIV

_____
_____
_____
_____
_____
_____
_____
_____
_____
_____
_____
_____
_____
_____
_____
_____
_____
_____
_____
_____
_____
_____
_____
_____
_____
_____

TODAY'S DATE: /   /

TODAY'S DATE: / /

Don't be afraid of making mistakes.
You can fail without being a failure –
it's all part of His grand design to take you to the next level.

_____
_____
_____
_____
_____
_____
_____
_____
_____
_____
_____
_____
_____
_____
_____
_____
_____
_____
_____
_____
_____

TODAY'S DATE: /   /

TODAY'S DATE: /   /

*"Peace I leave with you; my peace I give you.
I do not give to you as the world gives.
Do not let your hearts be troubled and do not be afraid."*
John 14:27 NIV

_____
_____
_____
_____
_____
_____
_____
_____
_____
_____
_____
_____
_____
_____
_____
_____
_____
_____
_____
_____
_____
_____
_____
_____

TODAY'S DATE: / /

TODAY'S DATE: / /

*"It's okay to vote for you sometimes.
That's not selfish, that selfcare."*

_____
_____
_____
_____
_____
_____
_____
_____
_____
_____
_____
_____
_____
_____
_____
_____
_____
_____
_____
_____
_____
_____
_____

TODAY'S DATE: /   /

TODAY'S DATE: /   /

"Go," said Jesus, "your faith has healed you." Immediately he received his sight and followed Jesus along the road.
Mark 10:52 NIV

TODAY'S DATE: /   /

TODAY'S DATE: / /

"If strength is what you need, God will carry you through, may God bless the fruits of your labor and everything you do."

TODAY'S DATE: /   /

TODAY'S DATE: /   /

"Therefore I tell you, whatever you ask for in prayer, believe that you have received it, and it will be yours.
Mark 11:24 NIV

TODAY'S DATE: / /

TODAY'S DATE: /   /

"It's not about being perfect, but living life with purpose, diligence, forgiveness, and repentance."

TODAY'S DATE: /   /

TODAY'S DATE: /   /

"'Nevertheless, I will bring health and healing to it; I will heal my people and will let them enjoy abundant peace and security."
Jeremiah 33:6 NIV

_____
_____
_____
_____
_____
_____
_____
_____
_____
_____
_____
_____
_____
_____
_____
_____
_____
_____
_____
_____
_____
_____
_____

TODAY'S DATE: / /

TODAY'S DATE: /   /

Being afraid doesn't mean you ignore God's instructions. Remember, He always give you what you need to succeed.

_____
_____
_____
_____
_____
_____
_____
_____
_____
_____
_____
_____
_____
_____
_____
_____
_____
_____
_____
_____
_____
_____
_____

TODAY'S DATE: / /

TODAY'S DATE: /   /

"Cast your cares on the lord and he will sustain you; He will never let the righteous fall."
Psalm 55:22 NIV

TODAY'S DATE: /   /

TODAY'S DATE: /   /

Don't allow your fears to be stronger than your faith, believe in the plans God has for you.

TODAY'S DATE: / /

TODAY'S DATE: / /

"Let the peace of Christ rule in your hearts, since as members of one body you were called to peace. And be thankful."
Colossians 3:15 NIV

TODAY'S DATE: /   /

TODAY'S DATE: / /

"Fear Not" is a command from God, not a suggestion.

TODAY'S DATE: / /

TODAY'S DATE: / /

"God is within her; she shall not fall; God will help her at (the) break of day." **Psalm 46:5 NIV**

TODAY'S DATE: / /

TODAY'S DATE: / /

Your beliefs are mental scripts that direct the show of your life; delete doubt from the script and watch your life transform.

_____
_____
_____
_____
_____
_____
_____
_____
_____
_____
_____
_____
_____
_____
_____
_____
_____
_____
_____
_____
_____
_____
_____
_____

TODAY'S DATE: / /

TODAY'S DATE: /   /

"Dear friend, I pray that you may enjoy good health and that all may go well with you, even as your soul is getting along well.
3 John 1:2 NIV

TODAY'S DATE: / /

TODAY'S DATE: /   /

If you only need faith the size of mustard seed to move mountains, imagine what doubt the same size can do?

TODAY'S DATE: / /

TODAY'S DATE: /   /

"Let us not become weary in doing good, for at the proper time we will reap a harvest if we do not give up."
Galatians 6:9 NIV

TODAY'S DATE: / /

TODAY'S DATE: / /

*Revisit the track record of God's unfailing love for you.
He came through 100% of the time*

TODAY'S DATE: /   /

TODAY'S DATE: /   /

"Blessed is she who has believed that the Lord would fulfill His promise to her." **Luke 1:45 NIV**

TODAY'S DATE: / /

TODAY'S DATE: /   /

You cannot be a prayer warrior and a praying-worrier at the same time. Have faith that all things will work together for your good.

_____
_____
_____
_____
_____
_____
_____
_____
_____
_____
_____
_____
_____
_____
_____
_____
_____
_____
_____
_____
_____
_____
_____

TODAY'S DATE: /   /

TODAY'S DATE: /   /

"Yes, my soul finds rest in God; my hope comes from Him."
Psalm 62:5 NIV

TODAY'S DATE: /   /

TODAY'S DATE: /   /

Hope is the down payment for God's promises of a bright and blessed future.

_____
_____
_____
_____
_____
_____
_____
_____
_____
_____
_____
_____
_____
_____
_____
_____
_____
_____
_____
_____
_____
_____
_____
_____

TODAY'S DATE: /   /

TODAY'S DATE: / /

"For nothing is impossible with God." **Luke 1:37 NIV**

Made in the USA
Monee, IL
24 June 2023

36774408R00089